Free Verse Editions

Edited by Jon Thompson

THE VISIBLE WOMAN

Allison Funk

Parlor Press
Anderson, South Carolina
www.parlorpress.com

Parlor Press LLC, Anderson, South Carolina, 29621

Printed in the United States of America
S A N: 2 5 4 - 8 8 7 9

Library of Congress Cataloging-in-Publication Data on File

Names: Funk, Allison, author. | Thompson, Jon, editor.
Title: The visible woman / Allison Funk ; edited by Jon Thompson.
Description: Free Verse Editions. | Anderson, South Carolina : Parlor Press, [2021] | Series: Free verse editions
Identifiers: LCCN 2020046433 (print) | LCCN 2020046434 (ebook) | ISBN 9781643171937 (paperback) | ISBN 9781643171944 (pdf) | ISBN 9781643171951 (epub)
Subjects: LCGFT: Poetry.
Classification: LCC PS3556.U62 V57 2021 (print) | LCC PS3556.U62 (ebook) | DDC 811/.54--dc23
LC record available at https://lccn.loc.gov/2020046433
LC ebook record available at https://lccn.loc.gov/2020046434

978-1-64317-193-7 (paperback)
978-1-64317-194-4 (pdf)
978-1-64317-195-1 (ePub)

1 2 3 4 5

Cover art by Louise Bourgeois. UNTITLED, 2006 (detail). Drypoint on cloth mounted on fabric. 17 ¾ x 14 ⅜"; 45.1 x 36.5 cm. Photo: Christopher Burke. ©The Easton Foundation / VAGA at Artists Rights Society (ARS), New York
Book design by David Blakesley.

Parlor Press, LLC is an independent publisher of scholarly and trade titles in print and multimedia formats. This book is available in paperback and ebook formats from Parlor Press on the World Wide Web at http://www.parlorpress.com or through online and brick-and-mortar bookstores. For submission information or to find out about Parlor Press publications, write to Parlor Press, 3015 Brackenberry Drive, Anderson, South Carolina, 29621, or email editor@parlorpress.com.

in memory of George,
for whom I was always visible

Contents

III

The Visible Woman

I

Against Vanishing

Afraid she is about to vanish
        I summon her
rib by rib, scapula, tibia,
        knowing how perfect she is
inside where she cannot see.

        Descend, I say,
into the heart's four chambers
        or the vestibule of your inner ear—
through its intricate labyrinth, hear
        how you hear so clearly,

word for word, pizzicato and bow.
        Clavicle, sacral, I whisper,
notes I want her to savor,
        but she turns and speeds away
like someone fleeing fire

        though I appeal to the rivers
that course through her blood, her brain,
        even her honeycombed bones.
Remember your earth, your mineral self
        I call—

you're not naught-nil-none,
        though small now as an ovum, pin-little
through the telescope I've become.
        Dimming, then brightening, you are
the variable star I set my sights on.

Cursive

Squinting at her faded signature,
I make out the careful loop of *l*
and *l* again, like a needle's eye
or the slit she slipped through
to get here.
With my poor vision,
though, how can I be sure I'm seeing her
as she was, and not as a schoolgirl
I've called on to stand in for me?
Blurred,
she's at her desk one moment
studiously bearing down between the lines
and the next she's working as hard
to erase what she's written
as she will
to rub herself out in time.

Once

after "Moll," a painting by Chantal Joffe

Once there was a girl small and bright as a crocus in the doldrums of winter or earliest spring. You know them, how they seem to be hiding in snow they push through to be seen. White, violet, involute, the tiny cups that open, emitting perfume strong enough to lure bees from their hives in February or March. Goldilocks, Venus, Joan of Arc, we can't help but name them. This one, the girl with yellow hair, dreamed herself tall—at least that's what the artist mused on a perch high above her studio floor splattered with petal-shaped pinks and blues. Not *pretty-pretty*—she'd never meant that—but when she turned to face the canvas face many times larger than hers the plot began to wobble. Who was—when—dissolving, along with her precious metaphor—what had started as a sprig, a slip of. Grown nearly ten feet tall, her creation nested, she could see now, in *blades* of grass. Down, down the scaffold, the artist knew she would fall, she was going to be crushed.

The Visible Woman

She's virtual as well as visible
    on a screen that lets me enter
through the gate of her ribs
    and fly so fast into her heart

I'm almost convinced
    it's pumping. Who knew,
inside, I'd find symmetries
    vivid as mandalas

monks create to erase.
    Mine, too, is a story
of how we disappear.
    Yet I keep returning

to The Visible Woman,
    the digital version scientists made
from flesh cross-sectioned,
    a feat unthinkable

in the nineteen-sixties
    when *my* Visible Woman arrived
in a kit of little plastic organs and bones.
    Thinking I was done with dolls,

my parents meant for me to recognize
    myself in this model as I grew,
even encouraged me to open
    the box of extra parts labeled *Optional:*

The Miracle of Creation.
    But faced with the enlarged breastplate,
pregnant uterus and thumb-sized fetus
    along with sheets of directions

(skeletal, respiratory, nervous, endocrine)
    I quit. Boxed up her vitals
and buried her at the back of my closet.
    Forgotten, she lay hidden for years

until, by accident, I found her
    and my way on the web
to her counterpart, where I discovered
    a woman's lungs bloom a deep rose.

The heart is stained a shade lighter,
    close to the blush of Mary's gown
in a Fra Angelico painting of the Annunciation,
    the one the girl forsakes to become

a Woman Clothed with the Sun.
    Queen of Heaven and Earth, Lady of Sorrows,
Mother Most Pure, Mother of Perpetual Help,
    the Mystical Body.

Icon, simulacrum, or the anonymous phantom
    who was once a real woman
from Maryland—I'm thinking again
    of how we're swept away,

and I want to go back to when I was ten,
    to start all over with the bones,
the brain, the heart in two parts
    I'm trying to glue together.

Blood

At the sight of blood, you'd think
he was Jonah awash in the putrid fluids
of the whale.
                    My father at sea
in his own body
scared me when he'd go pale, then darken
with anger, losing control.
                              And so I learned
to hide my wounds—scraped knees,
little playground injuries, even gashes
that needed stitching.
                          So long as I lied
when I bled, I lived apart
from the pain. Also pleasure,
that foreign address.

A History of My Skin

Just when I thought I'd finished
reading it, I discovered
a chapter I'd missed.
Similar, perhaps, to finding
one ancient text under another
on the untanned skins of calves
scribes reused, rubbing them
with pumice or lemon juice
until the original
nearly disappeared.

Still damp from a shower,
I noticed below my waist
between my left hip and navel
a little asymmetrical brown spot
that told me sun once shone there
long enough to leave its mark.
Wondering when that part
of me was last exposed
I doubled back to the sixties
and a bikinied teen

far from the cities that burned,
Harlem, Newark, Watts, Detroit,
those summers I was tanning.
By winter, my skin blank
as a baby's again,
I'd thought, no harm done,
as if anything could be erased.
Ignorance, my blindness.
Look, I think since. Find
what else you're hiding from.

Cells

after a series of enclosures by the artist Louise Bourgeois

Although *self* almost rhymes
with *cells*, I often feel I have
            nothing
in common with the body
I'm in.

~

I note how they divide, subdivide
as if under a lens—this thought,
            that emotion—
before art from chaos
can form.

~

Did my father survive in '45
because we unleashed the bomb?
            Because
we unleashed the bomb
I'm alive?

~

I hear church bells
tolling for those
            who wed
nights when the sirens
stop wailing.

~

When I thought my mother was dying
I saw she was me in a hospital gown,
            soft middle,

thin wrists, and I knew I'd be lost
if I lost her.

~

Secret, sliding, glass,
pocket, storm.
            Revolving,
barred, louvered, French—
I like to think of doors

~

as ports of call
where travelers can enter
            the unknown,
for the time being
putting their berths behind them.

~

The day the undertaker's men
lifted him onto a stretcher
            to ferry
my father away, I dreamed
he escaped through an unseen door.

~

Lift up your gates,
and you shall be lifted up—
            a plainsong
that heightens the longing
within my echoing chambers.

~

In an isolation cell
one can begin to hear voices.

I wish
this was something I did not understand.
This unfastening.

~

It's possible to break out
of a jailhouse or household,
although
most people tunnel away
inch by slow inch.

~

When I'm long gone,
with a view as wide
as Wyoming,
I might find myself
looking back

~

through a door left ajar,
half in love with the lingering
scent
of rooms as familiar
as the breath of ephemera,

~

hints of who'd lived there
in corners, on walls,
everywhere
except in the standing mirror,
which is blank.

Clemente Susini's Anatomical Venus, 1782

Though it's hard to read her face,
    those glass eyes half open
and rimmed with real human lashes,

    it's a breeze lifting her torso off
like a lid, no scalpel required
    to reach what's within

fashioned in colored wax—virgin—
    from Smyrna or Venice.
You count her ribs, the vessels

    and nerves made from fibers of silk
and fine linen, then dive straight
    into the abdomen's basin, sort liver

from spleen, locate the bean-shaped
    kidneys and unspool the entrails
as if naming her parts

    will help you fill in the thin
chalk outline you've drawn
    of yourself. Drawn and erased

for as long as you can remember.
    Thyself, how will you know
her? The one you're looking for

    in Susini's splayed mother in pearls
when you dead-end at her uterus
    fat with a six-month fetus.

Divine symmetry indeed,
    you whisper under your breath,
all the time wanting to believe

in the body's perfection,
as the artist must have,
needing to trust

your own articulated hands—
their branching of phalanx
and tendon, right the left's twin—

as you examine what you've found
with the care of a surgeon
closing a wound.

Watercolor

The painter choosing watercolor has gone under. *One Mississippi, two Mississippi*, how long does she have before what's seen is *un*, so quickly must she capture her subject at rest, soft-bodied as a medusa, lucent, long-armed, adrift. Sea-blue the blue she's in, see-through the watery hues the artist gives the model she dreams is dreaming herself a girl, a bell among bells in a bloom of moon jellies until, *three Mississippi, four*, she'll move, which she must soon enough, move like a fugue trailing herself before the woman puts down her brush.

Vespers

This late I'm still not in the body
  I'm trying to occupy.
No more *there* than the owls
  real only in the ruckus
they make at night—
  try catching sight of one
by day. Just once overhead
  I felt a gust, a sudden coolness,
and glimpsed a shadow cast
  in passing. Elusive
as the cricket in my house
  that stops shrilling
when I darken the stairs.
  (As if my airiness
could change a thing.)
  Downstream, downwind
of water falling
  from a height,
its *forte, fortissimo,*
  fortississimo,
I can hardly hear the lub-dub
  of my heart.
Gorgeous fury
  I'm outside of.

In the Studio: A Meditation

At rest in the gloam, I silently
 repeat to myself: hand, thumb,
second finger, third, fourth,
 and as my mind alights on
eyes, nose, mouth, cheeks, chin,
 I picture the separate stars
between which lines are drawn
 to create constellations—
Virgo, Andromeda,
 and Cassiopeia, the proud queen
I think of when the voice guiding me
 arrives at *whole body. Whole body*,
she says again. *I am.*
 For being a woman sure of her beauty,
Cassiopeia was condemned
 to tumble through the night sky
shackled to her throne:
 a cautionary tale for girls.
Here, though, the voice in the room,
 gentle, confident, nearly motherly,
tells a different story.
 Imagine, she says, a deep well
and yourself as a pail
 lowered slowly down.
When nothing separates
 you from the dark
I'll haul you up, brimming.

II

The Good Mother in the Art of Louise Bourgeois

They're all here, the women she's come from,
although the artist named her Good Mother alone.
See through gossamer thin as a scrim
her ghostly House Woman, Knife Woman,
even a reckless, youthful Athena at her loom
beating the weft into a shield and a spear, helmet,
then breastplate. I dare you! she shrieks,
to which, weaving faster, Arachne answers
for all the victims of tricksters, for those lusted after.
Beware the bull, the swan. A shower of coins.
At what cost do we make art?
you wonder, knowing Arachne, the contest's winner
and loser, came close to putting her head in a noose.
But see, hanging here, on linen
how indelibly she imprinted herself: the spider
the woman Arachne became. The mother. Us.

Chimera

Microchimerism occurs when cells from a fetus she's carrying migrate into a mother's body, where they can last a lifetime.

You could call me a hybrid, inhabited
By others clamoring in my blood—ancestors
And offspring, who've outstayed their welcome.
For years they have whined in my mind,
Kept time in my heart, making me wild
Enough to bleat in the key of a hungry goat.
Mark my territory as lions do in decibels.
My pride versus my *pride* at stake.
Most dangerous fenced, I can scare
Myself as the snake I am too, whip
That coils inside, going round and around.
Some days it takes all my strength to keep it
From leaving my mouth as fire.

In Daguerreotypes

It surprised me to find women
    pretending they weren't there,
but like her male counterpart

    in the nineteenth century
a lady photographer must have been
    used to camouflaging mothers

in portraits of their children.
    She'd even assist in shrouding them,
so a seated mother hidden

    under a blanket could keep a child
on her lap from moving
    for as long as light took

to darken a camera's plate.
    Still, I wonder what the photographer thought
when she disappeared

    beneath her own black cloth,
acting as if she couldn't hear the minor key
    mothers hummed

under their stifling folds,
    didn't notice their air of lavender
and curdled milk.

    Later, in the darkroom,
when erasing a peek-a-boo finger,
    the trace of a shoulder or wrist,

wouldn't she have been haunted
    by her sisters in the art
of now-you-see-me, now-you-don't

    as I am from frame to frame,
their effaced and misshapen
    forms all I see?

How We Are Silenced

If only words were charms and mine of use—
but no one can rouse her, not even a family praying
over their daughter face down on a mattress
in a makeshift house. It's been days
since she clambered through Mosul's rubble
to escape her captors after years
of bondage. Just sixteen, she fell
into her mother's arms, but hours later,
closed her eyes and stopped speaking.
Sometimes a person has to sever
body from being—
how else could she have borne the slurs?
The smothering men.
Back, she's a girl again in her mother's eyes.
No, hers is the sleep of the unborn
before they cry themselves alive.

Remembering Francesca Woodman

When I'm feeling far from my body,
I remember how you kept yours, always,
in sight, Francesca, courting her,
much as she tried to evade your camera's eye—
blurring as she moved away, shrinking
into corners, hiding her face.
As if the lens you aimed at her,
intended only to capture her beauty,
resembled the end of a gun.
How lonely you must have been
to follow her into wintry rooms
where she'd flare, then fade, as matches do.
But longing kept you focused,
focusing. Even when she made her way
to an open window to escape your gaze,
you, loving her, joined her on the ledge.

A Nun's Prayer

from Psalm 22

My God my God

  why are you so far from   my groaning

my   cry

  many   encircle me

they open   their mouths

  ravening

and   I am poured out

  bones   heart   breast

they stare and gloat over me

  divide my clothes

O Lord

  save me from

my brothers

  who   eat

Spiral Woman

after Louise Bourgeois's "Spiral Women"

Insomniac, she tosses, turns every which way
until she's wound
in sheets she can't stop spinning inside—

there, where voices entangle, one son's with another's,
her father's bass,
mother's countervailing treble. *Ne te dépêche pas!*

someone cautions, but still she hurries, turning
the damaged
tapestries over in the tannin-rich river

before, tightly, tighter, she squeezes all the water she can
from the wool.
Spiral Women, she calls the figures in her studio,

the ones she's shaped to revolve in the wind
the casement lets in.
Some nights she'd swear she overhears them whisper

of wringing the neck of someone who's wronged them.
Or is it
the workers in her mother's atelier, the weavers

she heard as a girl, sharing secrets of their art?
How they interlaced
indigo with rose madder from their unraveling skeins,

salvaging remnants of battles lost and won, scraps
of forest or garden
to create a whole cloth out of what was in pieces.

Anatomista

Anna Morandi Manzolini, 1714-1774

With her round face, thick neck,
 and matronly waist, no one
would mistake her for the Anatomical
 Venus or the Slashed Beauty,
Clemente Susini's odalisques

 also fashioned in wax.
In her self-portrait, Anna Morandi
 looks studious, as she must have
in the laboratory
 where she opened cadavers,

then modeled what she'd found:
 the intricacies of a hand
or the six muscles of the eye
 radiating like starfish arms,
one for each child she raised.

 Anatomist, artist, here
at the Museo di Palazzo Poggi
 in a taffeta dress, poised
with a scalpel above a human brain
 we see her as she saw herself,

says our guide. *In her likeness,*
 find your own inquiring self,
she advises before leading us
 into the next room
and the next in the palace.

Murmurations

Moving as one body,
        the way girls in matching suits
and caps practice figures in a pool,
        holding hands, kicking in unison
to create a flower or eight-pointed star,

        flocks of starlings synchronize in the air,
clouds of them morphing as they veer
        and dip and weave, wing-swimming,
though not for sport. Rather
        to escape a threatening falcon or hawk.

Don't underestimate them as some do
        beautiful women.
In seconds they can change direction.
        Swarm. Become a mass
that renders a predator helpless.

A Ghazal Written After Reading a Notebook Kept by Louise Bourgeois

A good mother needs a bad, a seamstress her thread.
Stitch a wife to mistress, imagine that thread.

What's more, she claims, pain is the business she's in.
To get out of her mess she'll follow a thread.

It's an art, she says to the doctor she sees.
How women sew codes into dresses with thread—

their SOS written in stitches and knots.
At home, distressed, she measures and cuts her thread.

Cross-stitch, back-stitch, split-stitch, darn. For crewel work
she selects a large-eyed needle. Tests the thread.

With a good worsted, she'd repair the damage
done by others. Her own. Forgiveness is the thread

she wants to weave throughout, though mostly it hides
in a seam, while anger surfaces, a long thread.

Fear glimmers, silver-gilt. She thinks it's her key.
In truth, she confesses, she confuses *fil*

with *fille,* the girl she was in France. A spider
and her web. When stressed, she holds fast to her threads.

At ninety, she'll make a book from remnants of linens,
pages of scarves and pale dresses bound with thread.

She calls it Ode to Forgetting, and, poet-like,
writes "return of the repressed" in her reddest thread.

Circling

I

I'm walking the path of a labyrinth
as if traveling a recurrent dream, here
and not here, my mind mazy as the way in

past the blue irises, bearded
and Siberian, among the distractions
of ones so like tropical fish their buttery

petals swim in the undulant wind.
By summertime, in full sun, my shadow
moves ahead of me, turning round

and around, drawing me on. When it snows
and the stones arranged to mark the way
lie buried, I think of the blind, the to and fro

of the long stick they swing to navigate
a new sidewalk or unfamiliar ground.
And so I use my right foot like a cane,

tap-tapping every snowy mound.
I wonder at times what it would be like
to be here at night when the moon

is covered with clouds, no flashlight
to guide me. Would the pathways
in my brain ingrained over time

lead me as the blind are led some days
by a sighted companion? I wish
someone could tell me the way

through sadness, this web of anguish
I'm in. Keep walking. Forget
your intentions, she might say, shush,

sotto voce, and though I try to quiet
the buzz inside my mind
I still feel like one of those solitary

bees that nest underground.

II

They're not here in the flesh,
but they don't seem far.
I find other people in what they've left:

rain-drenched, faded, flotsam a mother
bird might snatch to build her nest.
Strung from the tree at the center

of the labyrinth: what unravels, knots.
A red ribbon. A string of worsted yarn
fixed to a tarnished silver locket—

inside of it, the face of someone's
son. And next to this, his dog tag—name
and number—hung, I imagine,

in peace or protest, the steel chain
looped twice around the neck
of a branch. A woman's pain,

or man's, living apart in objects
like the ring and key I glimpse
through leaves. To what am I wedded,

and when, how, if ever, can I rinse
myself of what adheres to me? I wish
for a charm, a little bronze box, for instance,

with a latch I'd unfasten to spill the ash
each grief has become, to fling
it into the grass, the mum grass. Unlashed

I'd think. At last. But I've carried nothing,
my hands bare as a beggar's. Today,
come song, come night, circling

my concerns along the way,
I find myself where others have arrived—
if only some place

to rest for a while. How else do we survive?

III

How do we survive the dark
of the solstice, the short days of a long winter
where nothing harkens?

This little I know: the purple ash will be bare
before it buds. *Nowhere*
is a word I hear whispered

as the world gets colder. Also *prayer.*

IV

When a cool rain falls, what's within
blurs. I've given up counting the years
I've lived on a floodplain

where my house is endangered.
Stay, I say to myself, knowing
the smallest slip can trigger

it—tick tock and I'm drowning,
all the signposts submerged,
my door about to swing

off its frame. What calls me to emerge?
The heady scent of hyacinth. An iris
like a hand extended from the verge

of a past I thought I'd lost? A place
I went to be alone. In the temple
of Apollo, the gods created a sacred space

around the omphalos stone: navel
at the core of their world. *Axis mundi.*
Now, in the dream I'm having, mournful

strangers arrive in procession, wheeling
one around another before I recognize her
and her in the chorus forming near me—

Jane, who was Ursula's mother,
Denise, who was John's, among those
I can't name, their numbers

swelling. They hold out photos,
class rings, medical IDs,
a child's plastic barrette shaped like a rose:

votives to hang on our tree,
these memorials to children they've lost,
and tokens, too, I believe, of empathy

borne toward me like gifts.

V

The contemplative promises what's cruel
will, in time, turn merciful.
When I was young, I wrote of what befalls

us, sensing they were inseparable:
being and falling. How little
I really understood of the puzzle,

though, until my son, who was ill,
tumbled through the dark, spilling
himself. Slim as a candle's

flame, guttering, the little breath still
in him. For a month I kept vigil,
waiting for him to stir in the penumbral

dusk of a hospital room, unable
to say what I hoped for. Delusional
for years, he was the captive of a will

apart from his own, his troubles
ones I'd tried to, but couldn't, untangle.
And then it was April.

Friends would call it a miracle.
Maybe. All I know is my gentle
child has returned to me. He smiles

now, and can love. I am grateful
that, increasingly, between two verticals
I'm able to see a fragile

gossamer bridging them. A spectral
web, invented or real,
trembling between the jonquils

and day lilies, the purple
hyacinths, hummingbird and honeysuckle,
any pair of tendrils.

And life in the middle fills.

VI

The path out is identical to the path in,
and yet, though I'm retracing my steps,
nothing looks the same. *Union,*

the faithful call this stage. To forget
myself, to unself, I listen
for honey bees in the baby's-breath,

November's geese in their noisy migrations.
Skin of mine! What I'd escape
if I could follow the formations

of another species: the figure eights
the bees make, geese in their Vs.
Instead I imagine I'm shadowing Dante

to hell's circles, the steps of purgatory
and the spheres of his paradise
before losing him in the Milky Way

that's home to us, the *spira mirabilis*
that coils galaxies and cyclones
much as it curls the pearly nautilus.

These days nothing seems random.
Oh! we say together
when we nearly collide, two women

circumnavigating the labyrinth. Sleepwalkers,
each in our separate trance,
we apologize, half-smile, and turn

aside to let the other pass.
And though I can't rest as geese can
in the updraft of another's wings, thanks

is what I feel for a companion,
for snowfall, birdsong,
branch and drizzle, in all its figurations

what glimmers in my going.

III

Interior

In the beginning, I drifted,
    a mote
in my sunless inner world.
    Think of the sea's deepest zone,
home for creatures
    filmy as spirits,
as me, when I was translucent.
    A mere grace note,
then eighth, quarter,
    halfway through I grew
till, nearly filling my body
    of water, I woke
to shards of speech.
    Outside, it was sleeting.
The fifties. So little time to ghost
    unseen.

Self-Portrait as Louise Bourgeois's *Femme Maison*

I may as well have a head
which is no head, but a house instead,

though my arms like anyone else's
point north or south. Below, I'm naked

as all the unfledged.
When I offer a hand,

it may be hard to say
whether I extend it in peace,

peace or treachery.
Some see it as a call for help

when I'm waving goodbye.
You wonder

what it's like inside,
if I live like a bird hooded at night,

all the day through
cooing *coo coo*?

I'll let you in on a secret—
tiny as my windows are

I can see out. See you
while, as we both know,

you can't see in. So
let me tell you about my rooms.

Come close.
Are you picturing miniature

chairs and canopied beds,
a dollhouse stove and sink?

Mine
is more like a funhouse

with undulating floors,
trap doors and dark corridors.

Most of the time I can't tell
whether I'm moving uphill

or down. And worst
are the mirrors

filled with strangers
I know I should recognize

as myself. But there
are so many of me!

You try
getting out of your head.

Portrait Missing a Self

On a bad day, I feel the ache
        of having been,
as if I've become a phantom limb.

Then it starts, serrated wave
        after wave,
everything dangerous, bladed:

the keen edge of a stair,
        a pill bottle's rim,
my plane about to go down

behind enemy lines
        or into a wilderness
in which ready, set,

even the arrows of trees
        are taking their aim
until I remember

the sea star in extremis.
        Which regrows
an arm. And the writer,

nearly done for,
        creating a likeness
to embody herself.

Self-Portrait Starting as a List

No artist, I start with a list: head
first, of course, then throat,
trunk, or what I call my middle
which, being female, rises in breasts.
What else but appended arms, hands,
and legs ending in feet?

Head. Throat. Middle. Breasts. Hands. Feet.
Already this inventory in my head
won't do. Better the outline I drew by hand
as a girl: penciled boundaries—throat,
wrists and the rest, my own. When my breasts
filled in, the image changed. Later, too, midnights

as a mother roused in the middle
of a dream. On my feet,
on my way, though half-awake, breasts
weeping. We all know the icon. Her head
bowed toward him. The newborn's throat
rippling as he swallows. Hands,

all of him, latched. Unhanding
is something else. In the middle
of old arguments, games played cutthroat,
I think of a gorge hundreds of feet
across, wind the only voice in my head,
the path up too narrow to walk abreast.

I'm about to make a clean breast
of it, empty the cups of my hands
and pour myself headfirst
into the blue of middle
distance when I hear a note as sure as footfall
start up the sheer flight of my throat

like a glissando along a cello's fretless throat.
In what part, mind, heart caught in my breast,
will I find the fearlessness I need to secure my footing
on any tightrope I'm crossing? Freehand
on a highwire in the middle
of nowhere I know, I repeat my charms—head,

feet, throat—
as I head for the other side—breasts,
hands—at large in midair.

Self-Portrait in the Nude

To understand what it would be like
        to remove my clothes
as painters do in portraits of themselves

        I imagine I'm the woman
who knows her body
        no longer belongs to the artist

who painted herself before she had children,
        before her topography was changed
by forces erosive as water and wind,

        and yet she goes on painting it,
the girdle of her earth that is now an etched terrain
        crossed with silver rivulets.

And hills, I want to say to her.
        Valleys. Then *hummocks*,
hot springs, *hoodoo. What is art about*

        if not depression? Uplift? Depression
again? At which she straightens
        the flesh of her shoulders and neck

to face me before I disappear
        into landscape,
my favorite state of undress.

Study with a Black Hole

When I saw a photo of a black hole
I wasn't terrified as I'd been in my childhood
nightmare of being buried alive. What others called
monstrous, the hole's power to swallow everything
around it, appealed to the controller in me.
More, though, I liked the idea of giving in to it
as we must when we realize we can do nothing
about a loved one's drinking or addiction.
Or a spouse's attraction to someone else, or
how our bodies betray us as we age,
or, or, after trying to visualize the spiritual,
ending up with an infernal spiral
55 million light years away. Oh,
freedom, just the same, to be a broken star
on the edge, poolside, about to fall right in.
Even the smartest astrophysicists aren't sure
what would happen next—whether I'd be
vaporized, sizzled, or something else.
Where's she gone? people might ask, but the me
who always had answers that weren't answers
at all wouldn't answer. Poof. Vanished.
I've thought how soundly I'd sleep
with those black-out curtains. Inside,
I imagine like a hurricane's docile eye—
not quiet, though, as it turns out.
Did you know a black hole emits
the oldest, longest, lowest note in the universe?
B flat 57 octaves below middle C.
Can you believe it sings?
It sings to me.

Reflections of a Would-be Saint

How long have I been lying here
like some Sebastienne recounting offenses
or the daily frustrations that needle me?
Memories, too, those stubborn splinters
lodged for years, not to mention the prongs
I've caught myself on trying to escape
what's enclosed me. (Like a barbed-wire
fence, I've whined.)

Your point?

Throughout my life I have softened
my edges, blunted my blade by worrying
I might hurt others. Voodooed
without fatal wounds, just punctures
that smart, then fester in me—
isn't it time to pluck out
the rusting arrows, stand up
and stake a claim?

Diptych with a White-Tailed Doe

I follow her script of prints
in new snow. Watch her gnaw
the rhododendrons down to stubble.
Or nurse her young, two
at a time in the undergrowth.
Something like hunger pawing
within draws me out
in search of her, half-hidden,
though rarely far. Most often
we come upon the other

unbidden in a clearing where,
twinned, neither of us stirs
until the wind picks up
the scent I can't wash off.
I tell myself she knows the signs:
how my gaze dulls, breath quickens.
Shivering, I'll turn away,
cross the lawn, close my door.
The house woman. Inside.
When not in sight.

Self-Portrait Inside a Labyrinth

My friend asks if it's true
I've traveled the path of a labyrinth

when the moon is full. A writer, too,
she knows poets are susceptible

to the tidal pull of words. How hard it is
to resist *Flower Moon*, *Strawberry* and *Sturgeon*.

And what of the moons naming the months
deer paw the earth and the corn is in silk,

when the limbs of trees are broken
by snow, or heavy with fruit?

When ice on the river lasts all day.
Meltwater's moon.

Believe. Geese will molt, a trail break
open. Everything's about to be

gathered in, we say, naming
our luminous body. Moon of empty days.

And so forth, like the labyrinth
where I find myself going around

again—glowing, gibbous, waning, new.
Full? Let's say it's true.

Late Sketch

It's how I dream my squeezebox

will stop,

that relentless accordion of lungs

slowing down to a few notes,

the tail end of a coda,

and the swirling mind

burning out like the last pinwheeling

sparks of fireworks

or sex,

that pulse so like a nagging friend

I've known since adolescence

and finally, finally outgrown.

Now

awake as I've ever been

I see us all moving on,

our own dark energy

forever traveling

between the spiraling galaxies,

far-flung streamers of gas,

starburst after starburst,

tidal tails sweeping past

nebulae that resemble our own double helix.

So even *after*

we won't be far from who we were,

though released

from the roller coaster

we'd been strapped to—

shoot-the-chute, loop-the-loop—

we'll be weightless

off the track and out of time,

fugitive,

free-falling,

streaking through oblivion.

Notes

"The Visible Woman": Renwal, an American toy company, produced The Visible Woman, an anatomical model kit popular with children in the 1960s. In 1995, the National Library of Medicine created a collection of anatomically detailed digital images from the body of an anonymous female donor for its Visible Human Project (www.nlm.nih.gov).

"Cells": Louise Bourgeois created a series of architectural sculptures she called "Cells." Each is a unique chamber containing objects of personal significance to her.

"Clemente Susini's Anatomical Venus, 1782": Eighteenth century artist Clemente Susini designed wax models of women called Anatomical Venuses to teach human anatomy. Other life-sized dissectible women created by his workshop include the Slashed Beauties and the Dissected Graces. Some are in the collection of La Specola, the Museum of Zoology and Natural History in Florence, Italy.

"Watercolor": This poem was written with Chantal Joffe's watercolor titled "Ishbel Reclining" in mind.

"The Good Mother in the Art of Louise Bourgeois": Louise Bourgeois titled numerous works of hers "The Good Mother." The one that originally inspired this poem is a digital print with fabric collage she made in 2007.

"Remembering Francesca Woodman": Francesca Woodman was a ground-breaking young photographer when she died at 22 in 1981.

"A Nun's Prayer": My poem is composed of the words I did not erase from the New Revised Standard Version of Psalm 22.

"Spiral Woman": This poem refers to Louise Bourgeois's early life growing up in France as the daughter of parents whose business was tapestry restoration. She made different versions of her Spiral Woman over fifty years.

"A Ghazal Written After Reading a Notebook Kept by Louise Bourgeois": Louise Bourgeois often made lists in the notebooks she kept over her lifetime. One entry from a 1995-96 notebook (LB-0827 in The

Easton Foundation's Louise Bourgeois Archive) lists various rhyming words, including *dress, undress, caress, seamstress, mistress, witness, confess, duress,* and *stress.* I used many of them in my ghazal, as well as a variation of a sentence from the same notebook: "The good mother needs the bad mother, like the light needs night, white needs black."

"Self-Portrait as Louise Bourgeois's *Femme Maison*": Louise Bourgeois created her first *"Femme Maison"* in paintings and drawings during the 1940s. She often returned to her theme of the "House Woman," sometimes in marble or fabric.

"Late Sketch": I was thinking when writing this poem of Louise Bourgeois's 2008 series *"À l'Infini"* ("To Infinity"), an installation consisting of 14 large etchings with selective wiping, watercolor, gouache, colored pencil, and pencil additions in the collection of the Museum of Modern Art in New York.

Acknowledgments

Grateful acknowledgment is made to the following journals in which a number of the poems in this book first appeared, sometimes in different versions: *Beloit Poetry Journal, Cincinnati Review, Crab Creek Review, Crab Orchard Review, December, Diode Poetry Journal, Free Verse: A Journal of Contemporary Poetry and Poetics, Image, New Letters, Pleiades, Poem: International English Language Quarterly, Poetry Northwest, Prairie Schooner, Sou'wester, The American Journal of Poetry,* and *U City Review.*

I am very grateful to Maggie Wright, Executive Director of The Easton Foundation, for inviting me to work in the Foundation's Louise Bourgeois Archive. I also want to thank the Virginia Center for the Creative Arts for providing me with a residency there. Thanks to the Mercy Center of St. Louis and the amazing Rita O'Dea for retreats and encouragement that nurtured my spirit. I appreciate the ongoing support of dear writing friends, including Jennifer Atkinson, John Burnside, Jeff Hamilton, Andrea Hollander, Joshua Kryah, Howard Levy, Cleopatra Mathis, Eric Pankey, Steve Schreiner, and Jason Sommer. For their generous guidance on the poems in this book as they were being written, I am indebted to Marjorie Stelmach and Jane Wayne. It has been my good fortune to work with Jon Thompson, the editor of Free Verse Editions, and David Blakesley, the publisher of Parlor Press. For his help in designing my book's cover, I am grateful to my son, Josh Reingold. Deepest thanks for my beloved George.

About the Author

Allison Funk is the author of five previous books of poems, including *Wonder Rooms*, from Free Verse Editions of Parlor Press. The recipient of a fellowship from the National Endowment for the Arts, the Samuel French Morse Poetry Prize, and the Society of Midland Authors Poetry Prize, she is a Professor Emerita at Southern Illinois University Edwardsville.

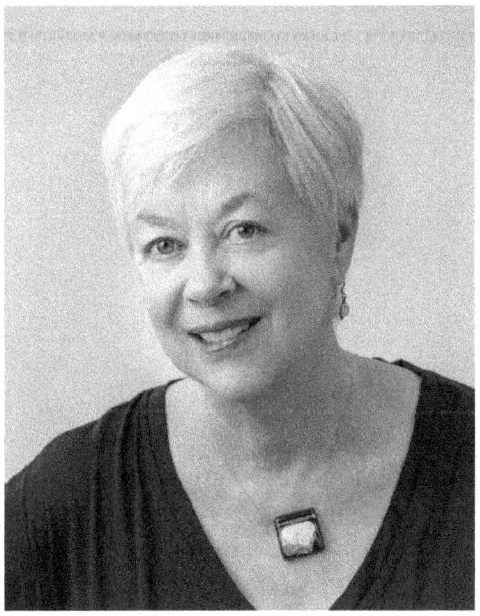

Photo of the author by Teri Dinnius. Used by permission.

Free Verse Editions

Edited by Jon Thompson

13 ways of happily by Emily Carr
& in Open, Marvel by Felicia Zamora
Alias by Eric Pankey
At Your Feet (A Teus Pés) by Ana Cristina César, edited by Katrina Dodson, trans. by Brenda Hillman and Helen Hillman
Bari's Love Song by Kang Eun-Gyo, translated by Chung Eun-Gwi
Between the Twilight and the Sky by Jennie Neighbors
Blood Orbits by Ger Killeen
The Bodies by Christopher Sindt
The Book of Isaac by Aidan Semmens
The Calling by Bruce Bond
Canticle of the Night Path by Jennifer Atkinson
Child in the Road by Cindy Savett
Condominium of the Flesh by Valerio Magrelli, trans. by Clarissa Botsford
Contrapuntal by Christopher Kondrich
Country Album by James Capozzi
Cry Baby Mystic by Daniel Tiffany
The Curiosities by Brittany Perham
Current by Lisa Fishman
Day In, Day Out by Simon Smith
Dear Reader by Bruce Bond
Dismantling the Angel by Eric Pankey
Divination Machine by F. Daniel Rzicznek
Elsewhere, That Small by Monica Berlin
Empire by Tracy Zeman
Erros by Morgan Lucas Schuldt
Fifteen Seconds without Sorrow by Shim Bo-Seon, trans. by Chung Eun-Gwi and Brother Anthony of Taizé
The Forever Notes by Ethel Rackin
The Flying House by Dawn-Michelle Baude
Ghost Letters by Baba Badji
Go On by Ethel Rackin
Here City by Rick Snyder
Instances: Selected Poems by Jeongrye Choi, trans. by Brenda Hillman, Wayne de Fremery, & Jeongrye Choi
The Magnetic Brackets by Jesús Losada, trans. by M. Smith & L. Ingelmo
Man Praying by Donald Platt
A Map of Faring by Peter Riley

The Miraculous Courageous by Josh Booton
Mirrorforms by Peter Kline
No Shape Bends the River So Long by Monica Berlin & Beth Marzoni
Not into the Blossoms and Not into the Air by Elizabeth Jacobson
Overyellow, by Nicolas Pesquès, translated by Cole Swensen
Parallel Resting Places by Laura Wetherington
Physis by Nicolas Pesquès, translated by Cole Swensen
Pilgrimage Suites by Derek Gromadzki
Pilgrimly by Siobhán Scarry
Poems from above the Hill & Selected Work by Ashur Etwebi, trans. by Brenda Hillman & Diallah Haidar
The Prison Poems by Miguel Hernández, trans. by Michael Smith
Puppet Wardrobe by Daniel Tiffany
Quarry by Carolyn Guinzio
remanence by Boyer Rickel
Republic of Song by Kelvin Corcoran
Rumor by Elizabeth Robinson
Settlers by F. Daniel Rzicznek
Signs Following by Ger Killeen
Small Sillion by Joshua McKinney
Split the Crow by Sarah Sousa
Spine by Carolyn Guinzio
Spool by Matthew Cooperman
Summoned by Guillevic, trans. by Monique Chefdor & Stella Harvey
Sunshine Wound by L. S. Klatt
System and Population by Christopher Sindt
These Beautiful Limits by Thomas Lisk
They Who Saw the Deep by Geraldine Monk
The Thinking Eye by Jennifer Atkinson
This History That Just Happened by Hannah Craig
An Unchanging Blue: Selected Poems 1962–1975 by Rolf Dieter Brinkmann, trans. by Mark Terrill
Under the Quick by Molly Bendall
Verge by Morgan Lucas Schuldt
The Visible Woman by Allison Funk
The Wash by Adam Clay
We'll See by Georges Godeau, trans. by Kathleen McGookey
What Stillness Illuminated by Yermiyahu Ahron Taub
Winter Journey [Viaggio d'inverno] by Attilio Bertolucci, trans. by Nicholas Benson
Wonder Rooms by Allison Funk

www.ingramcontent.com/pod-product-compliance
Lightning Source LLC
LaVergne TN
LVHW090545060426
835515LV00040B/1974

* 9 7 8 1 6 4 3 1 7 1 9 3 7 *